KELLEY R PORTER, CERTIFIED LIFE COACH

ALSO BY KELLEY (Kelly) R. PORTER

Perfectly Planned (Overcoming Incest, Rape & Sexual Abuse)

Perfectly Planned Audiobook

Overcoming Toxic Relationships (Creating Power from Past Pain)

Mental MakeOver (Creating a Positive Mindset) Book of Quotes

It's All About Life (Book of Poems)

Detox or DIEt (Closing the Gap Between Dis-ease and Death)

PERFECTLY Planned

OVERCOMING INCEST, RAPE & SEXUAL ABUSE
A Workbook and Guide to Releasing
Pain Associated with Childhood Abuse

"CELEBRATE LIFE AFTER ABUSE"

Kelley R. Porter

AWARD WINNING AUTHOR, SPEAKER & COACH

PORTER PUBLISHING
TRANSFORMING LIVES WORLDWIDE

Copyrights 2015 by Kelley Porter

Every effort was made to make sure that the information contained in this document is true and correct when released to press. However, the networks, systems, products, processes, specifications and content in general described in this document are subject to continuous development and Kelley is entitled to change them at any time and to expand on them. Kelley cannot accept liability for any loss or damage of any nature whatsoever arising or resulting from the use or reliance on information or particulars in this document. The information contained in this document is of a general nature. Should you need further advice for your particular personal requirements, please refer to the contact details below. No part of this document may be reproduced by any means, other than with the express written permission of the copyright holder.

If you require further information, services or products, please visit Kelley's website @
www.kelleyporter.com

Designed Kelley R. Porter
Cover Design by Kelley Porter
ISBN 978-0-9851767-3-0

Table of Contents

- Table of Contents
- Introduction
  - Purpose of the Workbook
  - Course Objectives
  - Course Outline

Table of Contents

Module I - Understanding Sexual Abuse and Other Forms
Module II - The Effects of Abuse
Module III – Conquering the Effects (R.E.A.R Technique)
Module IV - Move Forward in Forgiveness

Purpose of Workbook

The purpose of the workbook is to be a working document, reinforcing the information presented by the facilitator. This workbook is designed for use in conjunction with Perfectly Planned: Overcoming Incest, Rape & Sexual Abuse. The course is structured so that the facilitator refers to real life experiences written in Perfectly Planned in an effort to assist the reader in applying knowledge where necessary. Where relevant and possible, the participants then have the opportunity to complete exercises to consolidate their learning.

For more information about Perfectly Planned visit **www.kelleyporter.com**

Course Objectives

By the end of this course, you will be able to:

- Understand all forms of abuse
- Acknowledge and recognize the effects of abuse
- Release the effects of abuse
- Forgive your abuser(s) and move forward

Each survivor has unique experiences, feelings, thoughts, and ways of coping. With this understanding, it's possible for survivors of sexual abuse to find a peaceful resolution to very hurtful experiences. In fact, many survivors lead healthy, happy, and meaningful lives.

You will have the opportunity to provide feedback about the evolution of this workbook at the website address listed in the "About the Author" section.

Course Outline

Understanding Sexual Abuse
- What is sexual abuse
- The abuser
- The victim
- Who is at fault

The Effects of Sexual Abuse
- Lack of Trust
- Indecisiveness
- Poor Self Esteem/ Lack of Confidence
- Depression
- Compulsive Behaviors/Self-Medication
- Distorted View of Sex/Promiscuity
- Equating Love with Abuse
- Victim Mind-Set
- Guilt
- Shame
- Suicidal
- Pessimistic Mindset (Negative)
- Anger
- Fear
- People Pleaser
- Defensive
- Sexual Orientation Confusion

Conquering the Effects
- The **R.E.A.R** Technique
    - Recognize
    - Embrace
    - Accept
    - Release

Steps to Forgiveness
- Grieve
- Acceptance
- Understanding/Compassion
- Accountability
- Learn From It/ Find Something Positive

Those who have experienced child abuse are not familiar with how the abuse affected them as it is imperative that they learn and understand the effects in order to fully heal and find purpose in their pain. What's more, as adults and without the proper intervention, these individuals will live a lifetime with the victim mindset. The victim mindset prevents people from seeing their behaviors and understanding accountability and will ultimately prevent them from reaching their higher purpose in life. Within this guide, you will become empowered with the proper tools necessary to overcome your abuse, find emotional freedom and mental stability.

Module I – Understanding sexual abuse and all other forms.

In this module you will develop a keen understanding of what sexual abuse, who the abusers and victims are, and who is at fault.

What is your definition of sexual abuse?

_____
_____
_____
_____
_____
_____
_____

Were you ever sexually molested? If so, what acts occurred?

_____
_____
_____
_____
_____
_____
_____

How did you feel during this time of violation?

_____
_____
_____
_____
_____
_____
_____

Notes:

Sexual abuse: Unwanted sexual activities with offenders, making threats, using force or taking advantage of victims incapable of giving consent. Adults or older teens use a child for sexual stimulation. Forms of child molestation include asking or bullying a child into engaging in sexual activities; or to intimidate or groom the child; indecent exposure of a child's private parts to satisfy their own sexual desires, or using a child to produce pornography. Sexual abuse may include fondling a child's genitals, masturbation, oral-genital contact, and vaginal and anal intercourse.

Psychological abuse (emotional/mental): Non-physical behaviors such as threats, insults, monitoring; like excessive texting, and calling, embarrassment, pressuring, isolation or stalking. Also, when a person exposes another person to behaviors that are psychologically harmful, i.e. silent treatment, cussing, screaming, or when your parents, siblings, etc., degrade and physically abuse each other in front of a child.

Verbal abuse: Consistently degrading someone. It may take the form of angry outbursts or the "silent treatment" such as being cold, and calculating.

Physical abuse: The act of someone causing intentional physical pain, injury, or other bodily harm; i.e., push, kick, slap, bite, punch, etc.

Incest: Sexual relations between people closely related; the act of having sexual intercourse with a parent, child, sibling, cousin, or grandchild.

Use the area below to document your thought and emotions.

The Victim:
Were you under seventeen years of age when you were sexually molested? If so, how old were you?

_____

Did you tell anyone? Why or why not?

_____

Did you blame yourself? Why or why not?

_____

Kelley Porter
Notes:

_____
_____
_____
_____
_____
_____
_____

Note: Keep in mind, the consensual age of sex varies from state to state. For the purposes of this workbook, I am speaking to the state of Illinois as consensual sex begins at the age of 17. It may be different in your state. Please be sure to become aware of your state laws.

Victims of child molestation are innocent and this act committed against them is a sexual crime. In the United States, one in three girls and one in five boys were sexually molested before the age of 18. Sexual abuse happens across all colors, religious and socioeconomic groups. Unfortunately, sexual abuse is a common experience in the lives of children. Many countries around the world have become desensitized as it occurs more than statistics share. A report released by the National Institute of Justice in 1997 revealed that of the 22.3 million children between the ages of twelve and seventeen years in the United States, 1.8 million were victims of a serious sexual assault/abuse. There are gender differences with regard to sexual abuse incidents; girls are at twice the risk than boys for sexual victimization throughout childhood and eight times the risk during adolescence.

I urge you to look at this horrifying experience as just what it was; an experience. Do not allow this to destroy or control you any longer. Focus on removing yourself from the victim status by taking your power back. Tell yourself, "It's over; I am going to release this and become the beautiful and powerful person I am." Say that every day.

Use the area below to documents your thoughts and emotions.

The Abuser:
Did you know your abuser?

___

Was your abuser related to you? If not how were you connected?

___

How long did the abuse last?

___

Notes:

_____
_____
_____
_____
_____
_____

Statistics have shown that 90% of child molesters are familiar with their victims or know them in some way. Fathers are convicted of sexually molesting their daughters and sons as well as mothers. Uncles, brothers, sisters, cousins, babysitters, and friends of the family have all been convicted of sexually molesting a child. Child molesters are almost always someone you know and rarely a stranger.

According to the Survey of Inmates of State Correctional Facilities by the U. S. Department of Justice, more than half of violent offenders had victims age twelve or younger. The most common violent crimes by convicted sex offenders include the following:

- Fondling
- Child molestation
- Indecent practices
- Forcible rape
- Manslaughter
- Forcible sodomy
- Statutory rape
- Lewd acts with children
- Other sexual assaults

Use the area below to documents your thoughts and emotions.

Who is at fault? See Chapter 7
Do you believe the abuser is at fault? If not, why?

_____
_____
_____
_____
_____
_____

Were you blamed for being sexually molested? If so, how did it make you feel?

_____
_____
_____
_____
_____
_____

Do you still believe the abuse was your fault? If so, please explain?

_____
_____
_____
_____
_____
_____

Notes:

_____
_____
_____
_____
_____
_____

The abuser is **ALWAYS** at fault.

- There is no way a child is responsible for being sexually molested.
- There is no way a child can be at fault when an adult or older teenage violates him or her.
- Children and teenagers under seventeen years of age cannot consent to sex.
- It is natural for the body to respond in a pleasurable way when it is sexually stimulated, such as; erection of the genitals, ejaculation, lubrication from the vagina, erection of nipples.
- Even if your parent, sister, brother or cousin blamed you, the abuse was NOT your fault.

Find an image of you at the time you were sexually molested and paste it in the box. Look at it and then ask yourself two questions

1. How could that little person be responsible for being sexually molested?
2. How could you have known what you were doing?

Module II - The Effects of Sexual Abuse

In this module you will become familiar with the effects of sexual molestation and will be able to identify how the abuse affected you. The list provided are the ones I personally experienced after being abused. Sexual abuse causes a range of after effects, patterns and behaviors that children, teenagers, and adult survivors suffer from. I will not stereotype survivors of sexual abuse and expect them to have all or certain characteristics. My goal is to help you identify how the abuse affected you.

Inability to Trust:
Do you trust other people? Please explain your answer.

_____
_____
_____
_____
_____
_____
_____

Do you allow people to get close to your heart? Please explain your answer.

_____
_____
_____
_____
_____
_____
_____

Are you prepared to trust others when they give you no reason to distrust them? Why or why not?

_____
_____
_____
_____
_____
_____
_____

Notes:

_____
_____
_____
_____
_____
_____
_____

During sexual abuse, your life is interrupted with lies, betrayal and deceit. Children do not understand the concept behind trust, and do not have the mental ability to decide who can or cannot be trusted. Although, they may exhibit behaviors that's clear about wanting to stay away from certain people; they do not understand trust. When someone betrays a child, their perception of the world as innocent is no longer, and everything falls under deception. Without intervention such as God, coaching or therapy, meditation or prayer, one will grow up lacking trust for others. Listed below are a few things to look for to decide if the person is worthy of being trusted.

- Reliable- Doesn't break promises
- Honest- When someone tells you the truth, even if consequences follow; admitting to lies.
- Open- Answer questions in full details and not a simple yes or no.
- Volunteer information instead of being questioned.
- Loyalty- Their ability to be on your side, in your presence and your absence.
- Consistency in their behaviors as it relates to reliability.

Use the area below to documents your thoughts and emotions.

Indecisive:
Do you trust your decisions? If not, please explain why?

_____
_____
_____
_____
_____
_____
_____

Have you always trusted or distrusted your decisions? If so, please provide a scenario.

_____
_____
_____
_____
_____
_____
_____

Do you ask others if your decision was a good one? If so, what are you looking for?

_____
_____
_____
_____
_____
_____

Notes:

_____
_____
_____
_____
_____
_____

When children are sexually molested, in their minds they somehow believe they were responsible for this horrible act. When children believe the sexual crime committed against them is their fault it leads to them believing they made a bad decision. In turn, they lose faith and belief in themselves. That belief of being responsible for the abuse is carried throughout life and leads to not trusting their ability to make good decisions. Listed below are some ways to help improve your ability to trust your decisions.

- Pay attention to your body. Do you get a relaxed feeling or bad feeling in your gut?
- Listen to your heart, not just your mind. What is your heart speaking to you?
- Don't allow anxiety to set in from thinking too much; anxiety creates indecisiveness. Make the decision, good or bad, you made a decision.
- Don't ask others what they think. This is your decision.
- Rephrase the question so that your brain processes the information.
- Don't give in to temptation and make an impulsive decision.
- Weigh the risk and benefits of your decision.
- Remove yourself from those who try to persuade you otherwise.

Use the area below to documents your thoughts and emotions.

Depression: See Chapter 7
Do you understand the term depression? Is so, please provide your definition.

_____
_____
_____
_____
_____
_____
_____

Do you believe you are depressed? If so, please explain why?

_____
_____
_____
_____
_____
_____
_____

Have you ever been diagnosed with depression?

_____
_____
_____
_____
_____
_____

Notes:

_____
_____
_____
_____
_____
_____

Depression is a severe hopelessness, and unhappiness typically felt over time. Victims of sexual molestation are prone to suffer from depression due to the betrayal and pain, being blamed and/or feelings of being responsible. The violation is enough to make anyone depressed. Many times children do not tell even after the crime has ceased, and they carry the pain into their adult lives. If you have feelings of being depressed, I urge you to seek help. The list below accompanies symptoms of depression, but is not limited to.

- Anxiety
- Inability to sleep
- Overeating
- Loss of appetite
- Sense of meaningless
- Lack of energy
- Moody
- Feeling suicidal
- Social withdrawal

In my opinion, depression is the inability to process, manage and control your emotions. When we look at when one does not attempt to attack the challenges in their lives, we will then understand that emotions have the ability to dominate our mind, body and soul. I would encourage you to visit my website and register for one of my Transformational Coaching Packages.

Use the area below to documents your thoughts and emotions.

Distorted View of Sex/ Promiscuous: See Chapter 9

Do you understand the phrase Distorted View of Sex? If so, please explain. If not, try to explain it.

_____
_____
_____
_____
_____
_____
_____

Are you afraid to have sex? If so, please explain why.

_____
_____
_____
_____
_____
_____
_____

Are you, or have you ever been promiscuous? If so, please explain how you felt during these moments.

_____
_____
_____
_____
_____
_____
_____

Notes:
_____
_____
_____
_____
_____
_____

The term "Distorted View of Sex" refers to how one views sex. How an individual reacts to and copes differs from person to person. Instead of viewing sex as with two people who love each other, the mind becomes filled with painful thoughts. Love, sex and trust are important components of a relationship and sexual abuse destroys these components before the child reaches an age appropriate level to experience these things. Sexual molestation denies a child the opportunity to want sex and/or become interested in sex. In this way, the act of sex itself becomes distorted on when and how it is to take place.

Adult survivors may have many sex partners and lack the ability to say "no." Instead of understanding sex is between two people who love each other, adult survivors believe sex is not about love, and is about being used and treated as an object. In the act of being abused, victims trust their abuser and later in life, they confuse love, and abuse with sex. Adult male survivors view sex as power, and by applying that power he reestablishes his authority that was once taken during the act of child molestation. He also relates to sex as the most important part of a relationship and this leads to promiscuity.

Promiscuity is defined as having many sex partners without being selective or discriminating; someone who practices unsafe sexual behaviors. It's hard to pin down the exact odds of this happening to every victim of child molestation; however, studies have shown that promiscuity has a direct relation to child molestation. Many survivors who don't immediately get professional help may find ways to numb their pain. As mentioned earlier, some turn to drugs and alcohol; others engage in excessive sexual behavior, but causing more internal pain. Some adult survivors are left believing sex is a direct connection to love. Some also believe they are simply an object of pleasure and some use sex as a way to regain their power. Introducing children to sex can lead to sex addiction, while others have a difficult time saying "no." Focus on saying no and understand no-one deserves your body unless you are in a monogamous relationship with him/ her. Practice abstinence until you learn to love yourself.

Use the area below to documents your thoughts and emotions.

Equating Love with Abuse: See Chapter 5
Do you understand the phrase "Equating Love with Abuse?" If so, please explain.

_____
_____
_____
_____
_____
_____

Do you understand what love is? If so, explain your definition of love.

_____
_____
_____
_____
_____
_____

Do you know how to express and receive love? Please explain your answer.

_____
_____
_____
_____
_____
_____

Notes:

_____
_____
_____
_____
_____
_____

Love is not abuse. According to God, love is patient, love is kind. It does not envy, it does not boast, it is not proud. It does not dishonor others, it is not self-seeking, it is not easily angered, and it keeps no record of wrongs. Love does not delight in evil but rejoices with the truth. It always protects, always trusts, always hopes, and always perseveres. Love never fails. As a child you didn't know what love was so whatever your parents or abusers taught you, you believed. Victims of child abuse are born into abuse without any idea of what love is. There really is no confusion between love and abuse as it is the absence of love. As an adult, you may find yourself in abusive relationships as this is all you know. The goal here is to understand what love is and differentiate it with abuse. The bullets below list characteristics of one who understands abuse, but not love.

- If he/she doesn't hit you, you don't feel loved
- If he/she doesn't disrespect you, you don't feel loved
- Expecting certain behaviors, i.e. Name calling, hitting, aggression, constant chaos
- You provoke your partner intentionally looking for a negative response
- You feel a need to argue
- You are incapable of living in peace with your mate
- You say he/she loves you even after he or she hits you
- You consider them weak or too emotional when he/she shows you love & respect

Kelley Porter
Use the area below to documents your thoughts and emotions.

Victim Mind-Set:
Do you understand the phrase Victim Mind-Set? If so, please explain.

_____
_____
_____
_____
_____

Is someone always hurting you? If yes, please explain.

_____
_____
_____
_____
_____

Do you make excuses for your behaviors? If so, please explain.

_____
_____
_____
_____
_____

Notes:

_____
_____
_____
_____

The term victim mind-set refers to one who tends to regard him or herself as a victim of the negative actions projected onto them by others. What's more, these people speak and act as if something bad is happening to them **even when it is not.** These people reject help even when they are in trouble. The process of helping victim minded people is very painful. This mentality is a learned condition from family and situations from childhood, such as child molestation. As a child you were a victim, however, as an adult; you are responsible for your own actions. Without professional help, adult survivors will live a life of blaming others and never being accountable for their actions. The following list is a variety of behaviors and characteristics of someone who has a victim mindset, but is not limited to.

- Can't see the current situation for what it is; refuses to see what is happening at the current time and instead he or she blames and/or make excuses.
- Coping behaviors mimic the survival means used as a child. When disagreements arise, instead of dealing with the issue and finding a solution, he or she will withdraw, become angry or avoid the situation altogether.
- Reacts to current situations as if the abuse is happening. Instead of dealing with a situation with a positive attitude or recognizing your wrongdoings, you behave like the abuse is happening.
- Doesn't recognize their wrongdoings; instead of apologizing for wrongdoings one will dismiss the action as if it never occurred.
- Blame Game; it is never his or her fault. It is always someone or something's fault, i.e., the tree, the car, my mother, my job, etc.
- Assumes people are always out to hurt them; instead of perceiving constructive criticism as a way to help, they assume or accuse you of doing something wrong to them.
- Hurts those who are trying to help them – self explanatory
- Inability to explain their self-destructive behavior

    - Eating disorders
    - Alcohol and drug abuse
    - Failure to acknowledge their feelings
    - Lack of self-respect
    - Self-criticism
    - Sabotaging good relationships
    - Self-hatred
    - Bodily neglect

- The person feels there is something bad within their life, and whatever it is, it needs controlling or to be kept in silence. To remember this part of self is too painful as it reminds them of past experiences such as child abuse.
- Make difficult situations look like they are a victim. Victim minded people view tension situations as an attack on them even if they caused the tension.
- Inability to deal with life's situations' positively. When a problem arises, a victim minded person responds with negativity, i.e. anger, and negative body language, negative responses.

- Plays the "poor me" card; something always happens to them. They make comments such as, "why me" "why am I always being hurt."
- Refuse responsibility for their actions when things go wrong. They argue, ignore you or just refuse to apologize.

Use the area below to documents your thoughts and emotions.

Guilt/Shame: See Chapter 7 &12
Do you understand the terms, guilt and shame? If so, please explain.

___

Did someone make you feel guilty or ashamed about being abused? If so, please explain.

___

Are you ashamed of being abused as a child? If so why?

___

Notes:

Guilt is as an emotional experience that occurs when a person realizes or believes, he or she violated his or her own standard, a moral standard or societal conduct, and accepts responsibility for the damage. Understanding the term "guilt," adult survivors of sexual molestation should never consume self with guilt. Consider the fact that you were never responsible for being molested. The guilt arises from being blamed and manipulated into believing it was your fault. During sexual molestation and regardless of what your mind thinks, your body will become stimulated. However, that does not mean you did something wrong. It is a natural response when the body reacts to pleasure. You cannot control that. Lastly, abusers shift the blame or guilt onto the victim by saying "you liked it" or "you're getting wet or erect." That is their way of tricking you into believing you enjoyed being molested, and/or wanted it. In reality, abusers know the shame and blame belongs to them. Now that you understand where the guilt comes from, I urge you to remove the guilt and focus of forgiveness.

Shame is a painful emotion of humiliation or suffering caused by committing a conscious or thoughtless behavior. As you review and understand the term shame, I hope you realize being sexually molested carries no conscious behavior. A conscious behavior means you were aware of what you were doing. Did you make the choice? What's more, a thoughtless behavior is one committed without care and very selfish. Did you give any thought to being sexually molested? Victims of sexual molestation are hence the word, victims. The shame belongs to the molester as he or she knew exactly what he or she was doing. Child molesters know their behaviors are thoughtless, careless and criminally premeditated. The shame is what prevents the survivor from speaking out as in your heart you believe "you were a bad person" for what happened to you. It is commonly felt when you are certain someone will think bad of you for what happened to you. I want you to really focus on understanding the term shame as it does not belong to you. If you have never shared your experience with anyone, today is the day to stand up and speak out.

Use the space below to document your thoughts and emotions.

Compulsive Behaviors/ Self Medication:
Do you understand what a compulsive behavior is?

___

Do you or have you suffered from any compulsive behaviors? If so, please explain.

___

How do these behaviors make you feel inside?

___

Notes:

Compulsive behaviors are defined as acts that are persistently repeated, but without leading to any real reward or pleasure. These behaviors are used to satisfy an internal drive and to continually push one to avoid the reality of pain. The repetition resulting from this drive is not helpful or useful and can lead to addiction. All addictions originate from an unconscious denial to face, and move through your pain and anger. All addictions start with pain and ends with even more. Whether you choose food, people, alcohol, illegal or legal drugs you are using something or someone to mask your pain. Once you realize and acknowledge you developed these compulsive behaviors to mask the pain, you can then work to remove them.

Self-Medication:

Self-medication is a term used when we use substances to sedate or mask our pain. In reality, it only works while you are under the influence. However, as soon as the intoxication or "high" is dissolved the pain re-appears. As a matter of fact, the pain never goes away. Self-medication is a temporary fix for a problem leading to a more intense and dangerous addiction. After sexual molestation, most people develop a drug or alcohol addiction to escape the pain, but later in life, it becomes an addiction. Now you have two problems. Using a controlled substance to cut the pain is never the solution. If you have found yourself depending on liquor or drugs to deal with life, I urge you to seek help. Your alcohol or drug addiction is a symptom of the real problem; abuse and it will be there until you face and release it.

Sex or Hyper-sexuality
- Obsessed with sexual thoughts, feelings or behaviors

Overeating
- Eating uncontrollable even when not hungry
- Eating faster than normal
- Eating alone due to embarrassment
- Preoccupied with body weight
- Weight gain/instabilities
- Withdraw from activities due to being overweight
- Feeling guilty after overeating
- Eating small portions while dining out, but still overweight
- Aware of bad eating habits

Drugs/Alcohols - Addiction is a compulsive condition that causes one to pursue the substance knowing the negative consequences.
- High tolerance: You need more to feel the same affects
- Loss of control: Use more drugs than you wanted to
- Can't quit: You have a wish to stop, but can't
- Neglectful: Family time, children, and activities are no longer a priority
- Negative consequences: Interfering with marriage, job and causing health problems, but continues to use

Over-the-counter medications/ Prescription medications
It is easy to use and become addicted to something you have easy access to.

Shopping- According to Healthline, shopping addiction is also known as a compulsive - buying disorder or compulsive shopping. It affects about six percent of the U.S. population. While many people enjoy shopping, or treat it as a recreational activity, compulsive shopping is a mental health disorder and can cause severe consequences for the addict.

Shopping addiction is the compulsion to spend money, regardless of need or financial means. The addict may be addicted to a certain product, such as clothes or jewelry, but he or she may also buy anything from food and beauty products to stocks or real estate. Medical experts believe that a compulsive shopper gets the same rush or "high" from making purchases as a drug addict gets from using. Once the brain associates shopping with this pleasure or high, the addict tries to re-create it again and again.

Hoarding- Difficulty discarding or parting with possessions because of an apparent need to save them. A person who hoards experiences anguish at the thought of getting rid of the items. They have an excess of objects, regardless of the value.

Picking skin- According to TLC, (Trichotillomania Learning Center), Skin Picking Disorder is a serious and poorly understood problem. People who suffer from SPD repetitively touch, rub, scratch, pick at, or dig into their skin, often in an attempt to remove small irregularities or perceived imperfections. This behavior may result in skin discoloration or scarring.

Gambling- According to the University of Texas, gambling addiction is a disease, similar to alcohol addiction, in that gamblers often lose control over their behavior and face serious consequences. For many people, gambling problems may increase gradually. Over time, gambling may:

- Become a way of trying to cope with or escape from life's stresses
- Contribute to impaired judgment and risky behaviors
- Isolate the gambler from others
- Lead to feelings of shame and lowered self-esteem
- Damaged or destroyed relationships

Use the area below to documents your thoughts and emotions.

Suicidal: See Chapter 7
Have you ever thought about attempting suicide? If so, what were your thoughts?

_____
_____
_____
_____
_____
_____

Have you ever attempted suicide and if so, how?

_____
_____
_____
_____
_____

Do you feel a desire to attempt suicide today? If so, please explain why?

_____
_____
_____
_____
_____
_____
_____

Notes:

_____
_____
_____
_____
_____

Suicide is the intentional killing of oneself. It is also a permanent solution to a temporary problem. Survivors of abuse usually think about or attempt suicide to block the unbearable pain. One who tries to attempt suicide is very depressed and cannot see any other solution to their problems. I urge you to seek help if you feel this way today or any day. I know all too well about suicide as I have tried twice and contemplated once. Today, there is nothing in this world that would make me want to take my life. I know the pain is unbearable, but in time and with faith you can and will conquer this.

How do you remove the thoughts of suicide?

- Admit it to your loved ones and seek help.
- If you have these thoughts, promise yourself you will allow two days to pass before any actions.
- Don't use alcohol or drugs as they will make your challenges seem worse.
- Figure out what makes you think about suicide. Why are you having these thoughts? Have you had these thoughts before?
- Talk to people who understand.

Use the area below to documents your thoughts and emotions.

Pessimist:
Do you understand the term pessimist? Is so, please explain?

Do you believe you have a pessimistic mindset? Why or why not?

Why do you have a pessimist mindset or attitude?

Notes:

A pessimistic person is one who is routinely low-spirited, and sees or anticipates the worst. When children are victims of child molestation, their first experience is life altering and negative. In the absence of intervention, one will grow with the same outlook on life; everything will end badly and everyone will be worse. What I want you to understand is your thoughts become things. The more you focus on negativity, the more negativity will present itself in your life. Focus on the positive.

How to remove negative mindset?
- Face and admit your shadow side or flaws. Write them down and think about where they originate.
- Find new friends. Hanging around negative minded people will rub off. Close associations bring strong similarities.
- Count your blessings. Each day you awake, write what provides you with happiness and gratitude.
- Ask your friends and family to tell you when you are being pessimistic.
- When approached with a situation that may provoke your negative mindset, ask yourself, what can I learn from this? How can I change the way I feel? Why am I feeling this way? Is there another way I can view this situation?
- Find something positive. There is always something positive in every negative. For instance; your boyfriend cheated on you and hurt your feelings. You left him and now do not have to worry about his cheating behaviors.

Use the area below to documents your thoughts and emotions.

Anger: See Chapter 6
Do you understand the term anger? Is so, please explain?

_____
_____
_____
_____
_____
_____

Are you angry? If so, please explain.

_____
_____
_____
_____
_____
_____

Why are you harboring anger?

_____
_____
_____
_____
_____
_____

Notes:

_____
_____
_____
_____
_____
_____

Anger is a strong feeling of annoyance, displeasure, or hostility; rage. Victims of abuse should feel angry since their innocence was stolen. I understand your anger as I have been there. I wanted to destroy everything and one in my path. I wanted to cause others the same pain because behind anger, lies pain. I get it, however, I do not want you harbor anymore anger. Anger is like a poisonous snake and each day you are angry, the snake bites you. The only person you are hurting is yourself. Your abuser has moved on to prison or to commit more crimes. Remember, your thoughts are the core of who you are and if you want to live in peace, you must change your thoughts.

How do you remove the anger?

- Ask yourself; is it really that important to respond immediately?
- Cool off; count to ten and take deep breaths.
- Think about where the anger is coming from.
- Analyze the situation. What is the big picture?
- Remove yourself from the situation.
- Don't bottle the anger. Come back later and express your feelings calmly.
- Understand you don't always have to be right.
- Find humor in the situation.
- Remember, everything will not always go your way.

Use the area below to documents your thoughts and emotions.

Fear: See Chapter 12
Do you understand the term fear? Is so, please explain?

_____
_____
_____
_____
_____
_____

What are you afraid of and why?

_____
_____
_____
_____
_____
_____

What can you do to remove this fear and replace it with courage?

_____
_____
_____
_____
_____
_____

Notes:

_____
_____
_____
_____
_____

Fear is feeling afraid; or showing anxiety. Believe it or not, you created these fears as a child and rightfully so. Any child violated by an adult or anyone for that matter will develop fears. As an adult you have no need to fear anything. Fear is simply a false expectation appearing real. For example, if you have to complete a term paper in school; you fear the results will be horrible so you don't attend school and/or refuse to complete the paper. In reality, you will never know what the results were since you never attended school or completed the paper. Think about that; you created that fear and all you had to do was apply yourself and not worry about the results. The worst thing you can do to self is allow the unknown to stop you from trying.

Listed below are some ways to remove and release fears?

- Acknowledge it; write it down; it is easy to deny or ignore our fears.
- Determine the basis of the fear. Is it related to your childhood or did it start with a negative experience?
- Determine how the fear affects you. Does it cause you to miss school because you are afraid of failing? Does it cause you to avoid relationships because you are afraid of being hurt?
- Tell yourself it isn't real. Generally, we develop fears of something because we are unaware of it. "Fear of the unknown."
- Envision the result you desire. Instead of defeating yourself, tell yourself this is going to be a great experience regardless of the results.

Use the area below to documents your thoughts and emotions.

Low Self-Esteem/ Lacking Confidence/Insecure: See Chapter 9 & 12
What is your definition of low self-esteem/ lacking confidence and/ or insecure?

___

Do you have low self-esteem? Do you lack confidence? Please explain your answer.

___

Do you believe you are insecure or lack confidence because you were abused? If so, please explain.

___

Notes:

Insecure means unsure of yourself; lacking confidence or uncertain of who you are. Insecurities are unfortunate self-doubts either originating from growing up in a dysfunctional household or being betrayed and deceived as an adult. The unfortunate part is the behaviors that surface from these insecurities are forced upon an innocent person and causes unnecessary pain. An insecure person is a vulnerable person easily molded by the opinions, and ideas of others. Insecure people are unsure about their values and beliefs, and more than often do not defend self. After being abused, you never developed into the "real you" because abuse interrupts your emotional growth and development.

Confidence is a feeling or showing confidence in oneself; self-assured. Lacking confidence is the opposite and goes along with being insecure; unsure. Sexual molestation or any form of abuse strips you of your confidence. Again, as stated within the insecurity section; abuse interrupts your emotional and mental growth, and development. Physically children grow into adults; however, their mental growth suffers a severe interruption that leads to a no emotional growth. The reason behind this is after sexual molestation, it is very difficult to move forward so your focus becomes what happens to you and not how to move forward. Listed below are some examples of being insecure or lacking confidence.

- Give reasons for your actions: If you make a mistake, you explain yourself.
- Immediately responds to criticism and aggressively even if it is constructive criticism. Confident people listen to criticism and accepts it if it's positive.
- Perfectionist: Tries to do everything perfect.
- Selfishness: Never willing to help others as they hide behind their accomplishments.
- Arrogance: Constantly telling others how much they have, what they have, and what they are good at.
- Body language: Head down, slumped shoulders, no eye contact when talking.
- Don't trust in relationships.
- Jealousy: Instead of being happy for others, you are angry or envy their blessings.
- Gossiping and back stabbing: A secure or confident person would never waste their energy on dragging others down.
- Extremely competitive: Always feel the need to show someone up, or out-do someone.
- Make others look bad: Humiliating others in public as a way to make you feel better.
- Compensate for your weaknesses by denying issues in your life or makes statements like "I'm always happy."
- Change your beliefs about self-image. If you believe you are ugly, change that thought as the right brain creates exactly what you speak.
- Understand that being secure has nothing to do with materialistic wealth. Your possessions may make you feel good for a moment, but what happens when they are gone?
- Don't compare yourself to what's in your mind. In your mind you may think you're a movie star, but when you compare your real life with your thoughts, it results in self-rejection.
- Think positive thoughts: Instead of saying you are not good enough, tell yourself you are too good to be true.

- Remove negative images and thoughts about self; see and know that you are a beautiful person
- Don't embrace what others think about you unless it is positive.
- Stop creating false images of self in your head.
- Remove the image of perfection as you will never be perfect; no one is.

Low self-esteem is lacking self-respect or love for oneself. All forms of child abuse will have a negative effect on a growing child's sense of self-worth. Although the different forms may have different effects, low self-esteem is a common characteristic among victims of abuse. Neglecting or abusing a child results in that child feeling unworthy of love or importance. As the child grows and is able to see how other parents treat their children and not in an abusive way, the child is able to decipher how families function and by comparison, the child believes he or she isn't worthy of love. Later in life, the child becomes a teenager, then an adult and carries those feelings throughout. Listed below are some ways to increase your self-esteem?

- Write down the positive and negative things about self; ten to fifteen each. You can't fix what you refuse to embrace or accept.
- Set realistic expectations. Instead of expecting to lose ninety pounds in three months, go for nine months to a year.
- Remove the negative thoughts as they directly affect your self-esteem. Instead of saying, I can't do this, say, I can do this.
- Remove perfection and be grateful for your accomplishments and errors. Never down-play your accomplishments and don't upgrade your mistakes.
- Don't compare yourself to others. This is a definite blow to your self-esteem. Self-comparison only.

Use the next page to share your thoughts and emotions.

People Pleaser: See Chapter 7
Do you understand the term people pleaser? If so, please explain?

_____
_____
_____
_____
_____
_____
_____

Are you a people pleaser and if so, how?

_____
_____
_____
_____
_____
_____
_____

How does it make you feel when you don't do what others want you to do?

_____
_____
_____
_____
_____
_____

Notes:

_____
_____
_____
_____
_____
_____

People pleasers are those who never say "no" and spend a great amount of time doing things for other people. This is very unhealthy. The desire to please others is deeply rooted in either a fear of rejection and/or a fear of failure. If you don't do something asked of you, you fear rejection or losing the person. If you make a mistake, you will disappoint people or be punished. Victims of abuse or those with highly critical parents will develop this behavior. People pleasers are self-neglecting. You also develop passive-aggression or resentment for others. You become silently angry towards the people in your life. This can become very stressful as eventually you will become consumed with anger and become implosive. What's more, people will take advantage of you.

Listed below and on the next page are a few behaviors that will assist you in determining if you are a people pleaser and ways to remove this behavior.

- Difficult to say "No"
- Avoid speaking your mind or rocking the boat
- Pretend you are someone else for the sake of others
- Avoids getting angry
- Settle with someone else's opinion and not expressing your own
- Unsure about what you want
- Difficult to express feelings different from someone you're close to
- Difficult to take initiative
- Suppressing your emotions for the sake of others

Listed below are some ways to remove being a people pleaser and become a self-pleaser.

- Learn how to say no. If someone makes a request of you that you do not want to do, just say no. Don't make excuses or think about it, just say "No."
- Voice your opinion. If you and some friends are going to dinner, but you want Italian and everybody else wants Chinese, say it. It doesn't mean everybody will agree with you, but at least you voiced your opinion and the next time your friends will remember. Ask for help if you need it. No one can read your mind. Asking for help doesn't mean you failed, it means you refuse to fail.
- Be yourself. If someone wants you to behave a certain way to satisfy their selfish needs, express your beliefs and stand strong in which you are. Be careful as to decide if the change is for them or good you.
- Do something for you. Do something you have always wanted to do and feared others would not approve. Like Nike says "Just Do It." Stop worrying about what others think. If you develop thoughts about what Mike or Sue might think, tell your thoughts to go sit down.
- If someone makes you upset, it's okay to express your emotions as your emotions are real. Remain calm and express yourself.
- Take initiative; regardless of the outcome. It is better to try than not try at all and not know the results. Do what your heart tells you to do. If you want to cook dinner and isn't sure how it will taste, cook it and find out. If no-one likes it, then more for you.

- Compromise; it is okay to listen to what others want, but if your heart disagrees, express that. However, do not become selfish. The goal here is to be certain that you're doing exactly what you want and not what others want you to do.
- Maintain confidence about your desires and don't let anyone change it. If you want chocolate ice cream and someone says you should have vanilla, don't take it. Get your chocolate ice cream.
- If the people in your life get angry or reject you for saying "no" get rid of them as they are only out for what they can get from you.

Use the area below to documents your thoughts and emotions.

Defensive:
Do you understand the term defensive? Is so, please explain?

Do you live on the defense? Why or why not?

What can you do to be less defensive?

Notes:

Defensive is very anxious to challenge or avoid criticism; oversensitive, paranoid, self-justifying. As it relates to children and abuse, children are rarely if ever taught how to protect themselves from more abuse. It is not the abuser's intent to teach a child how to protect themselves and in a home such as the one I grew up in with a passive mom, there was no protection. Children are often blamed and accused of being a liar. Suppose you told your mother there was a large dog standing on your front porch and you were afraid to go outside. Your mother then told you the dog was small, without teeth and to go outside and play. That would leave any child feeling unsafe and unprotected in the world. When a victim or survivor is silenced, doubted, shamed or left unprotected, these children who are now adults have developed their own way to protect themselves. They become defensive to protect themselves from future pain that is nowhere in sight. It doesn't matter if someone is offering constructive criticism; a defensive person can only see an attack as they fear being hurt again.

Use the area below to documents your thoughts and emotions.

Kelley Porter — Perfectly Planned Workbook

Sexual Orientation Confusion:
Were you sexually molested by the same sex?

Do you hate the opposite sex?

Are you lesbian or homosexual?

Notes:

There are so many victims of child molestation; men and women alike who live a homosexual or lesbian lifestyle. In my experience, being sexually molested by the same sex and forced to engage in sexual activities with the same sex created confusion about my sexual orientation. However, that did not make me a lesbian. It made me a hyper-sexual person. I slept with women for over ten years and when I decided to dig deep and understand where the desire came from, I made the connection. I realized my body enjoyed the sexual pleasures as a young child and never forgot. As an adult and like many, I acted on that desire and had sex with many women.

What's more, being sexually molested or abused by the opposite sex can create a fear and/or distrust in the opposite sex that might lead to seeking love and acceptance from the same sex. Sexual abuse not only confuses you about your identity, but it also creates sexual orientation confusion. Make the connection.

Use the area below to document your thoughts and emotions.

Module III – Conquering the Effects: The R.E.A.R Technique

The Internal Work
In this module you will develop an understanding on how the abuse affected you. You will recognize, embrace, accept and release these effects. This is your work and doing it will result in freedom.

Recognize: Recognize your patterns and behaviors.

I listed several patterns and behaviors associated with childhood abuse. Select the ones you feel affects you and then add those I have not listed. This requires your truth. If you decide to lie to yourself, the outcome will be the same. When you're honest, the outcome will change. I had to admit the previously listed behaviors in order for me to release them. Only you know how the abuse affected you and if you don't, I have provided many examples.

This work isn't easy as it took me eighteen (18) years after I discovered the truth for me to redefine and reveal my true self. However, everyone is different. Your journey is different from mine. The most important thing is to do the work. In this section, you will be honest with yourself and document all the patterns and behaviors you identified and stay conscious of them. Know that these behaviors are abnormal and your goal is to remove them. In life, you will come face to face with triggers, but your choices should be based on today and not yesterday. Once you have released your past pain and experiences, triggers will become obsolete as they will no longer be considered "triggers" since there will be no reaction to them. A trigger is only a trigger if the mind reacts and causes a behavioral reaction based on the emotions surrounding the trigger.

Before you move any further, document the behaviors, thoughts or emotions you live with as an adult. Then look back on your childhood abuse and discover where that pattern, behavior or emotion came from and write that down as well. Make comparisons. In other words, how did you feel about self as a child after the abuse and how do you feel as an adult today.

_____
_____
_____
_____
_____
_____
_____
_____

Embrace: Now that you have identified your patterns, behaviors and emotions, embrace them.

It is important to embrace these things as they are a part of you. If you refuse to embrace these emotions, patterns or behaviors, how can you embrace you? The purpose behind this is to help you understand that by embracing, you allow yourself to move forward in releasing them. It is when you refuse to embrace your truth; you will continue to live a lie. What's more, these patterns and behaviors are the effects of abuse and not something you want to hold on to; however, to release them, you have to embrace them. The only way out is through.

Previously, you listed how the abuse affected you and now I want you say them out loud, and understand they are the effects of abuse and NOT who you are. I want you to stop lying to yourself and know that the abuse not only hurt you, but changed you into someone you are not. I want you to admit how badly the abuse damaged you, and understand these effects have buried the person you really are. After you have completed this work, you will release them.

Before you move any further, read your emotions, patterns and behaviors out loud.
Complete this assignment on the next two pages.

1. Write an example of how **each** pattern, behavior or emotion exists in your life today.
2. Write an example of how this behavior interferes with, or affects your normal life.
3. Write an example of how these behaviors serves no purpose in your life.
4. Write an example of why it is important to remove these behaviors.
5. Write an example of how these behaviors are not a part of who you are.
6. Write an example of how your patterns, behaviors and emotions relate to your childhood abuse.
7. Write an example of how each behavior or emotion arises when there is conflict in your life today.
8. Write an example of how these patterns or behaviors are associated with triggers.

Kelley Porter

Now that you understand your patterns and behaviors are associated with your childhood abuse, remove them as they are only thoughts. And you are what you think you are. As I stated previously, the only purpose for embracing these affects is to so that you learn to stand in your truth resulting in creating a better person.

Listed below are affirmations taken from the stated website. This is what I want you to tell yourself now and daily as eventually you will believe them. Remember thoughts become things and if you think, speak and act positive, I guarantee a new you will arise.

http://www.huffingtonpost.com/dr-carmen-harra/affirmations_b_3527028.html

- I am the architect of my life; I build its foundation and choose its contents.
- Today, I am brimming with energy and overflowing with joy.
- My body is healthy; my mind is brilliant; my soul is tranquil.
- I am superior to negative thoughts and low actions.
- I have been given endless talents which I begin to utilize today.
- I forgive those who have harmed me in my past and peacefully detach from them.
- A river of compassion washes away my anger and replaces it with love.
- I am guided in my every step by Spirit who leads me towards what I must know and do.
- (If you're married) My marriage is becoming stronger, deeper, and more stable each day.
- I possess the qualities needed to be extremely successful.
- (For business owners) My business is growing, expanding, and thriving.
- Creative energy surges through me and leads me to new and brilliant ideas.
- Happiness is a choice. I base my happiness on my own accomplishments and the blessings I've been given.
- My ability to conquer my challenges is limitless; my potential to succeed is infinite.
- (For those who are unemployed) I deserve to be employed and paid well for my time, efforts, and ideas. Each day, I am closer to finding the perfect job for me.
- I am courageous and I stand up for myself.
- My thoughts are filled with positivity and my life is plentiful with prosperity.
- Today, I abandon my old habits and take up new, more positive ones.
- Many people look up to me and recognize my worth; I am admired.
- I am blessed with an incredible family and wonderful friends.
- I acknowledge my own self-worth; my confidence is soaring.
- Everything that is happening now is happening for my ultimate good.
- I am a powerhouse; I am indestructible.
- Though these times are difficult, they are only a short phase of life.
- My future is an ideal projection of what I envision now.
- My efforts are being supported by the universe; my dreams manifest into reality before my eyes.
- (For those who are single) The perfect partner for me is coming into my life sooner than I expect.

- I radiate beauty, charm, and grace.
- I am conquering my illness; I am defeating it steadily each day.
- My obstacles are moving out of my way; my path is carved towards greatness.
- I wake up today with strength in my heart and clarity in my mind.
- My fears of tomorrow are simply melting away.
- I am at peace with all that has happened, is happening, and will happen.
- My nature is divine; I am a spiritual being.
- My life is just beginning.
- I am God.

Love is patient, love is kind. It does not envy, it does not boast, it is not proud. It does not dishonor others, it is not self-seeking, it is not easily angered, and it keeps no record of wrongs. Love does not delight in evil but rejoices with the truth. It always protects, always trusts, always hopes, and always perseveres. Love never fails.

Rewrite the previous paragraph and place your name where the word "love" and "it" exists.

_____
_____
_____
_____
_____
_____
_____
_____
_____
_____

Accept: Now that you embraced your patterns, behaviors and emotions associated with abuse, you can now accept what happened.

What happened will not change, but you will if you do the work. Acceptance is the key in evolution as without it you remain in the same mental state. Those patterns, behaviors and emotions are buried in your subconscious mind and when triggered it is in that place you return to, and your entire life is based on yesterday, and not today. How do you accept something that caused you great pain and left you with instabilities and scars? Simple, you cannot change the act, but you can change your mindset. This means you accept your past experience as something that happened for you and not to you. Acceptance will guide you to freedom.

Say the following statement out loud.

"I was abused as a child and I accept it. The instabilities are not a part of my true self. These things are common when a child is abused. I will focus on being a victor and no longer a victim of my past experience."

Assignment:
Write an essay on why it is important to recognize and embrace the effects of abuse, and why it is important to accept your childhood abuse.

_____
_____
_____
_____
_____
_____
_____
_____
_____
_____
_____
_____
_____
_____
_____
_____
_____

Kelley Porter

Release: Now that you have recognized and embraced the patterns, behaviors and emotions, and accepted your childhood abuse, it is time to release the pain.

Doing the work means seeking the truth, living in your real truth and applying the truth to your life. Whether it is reading a book, or this workbook, watching an episode discussing abuse, meditating or praying; doing the work means you diligently work on living in your today. This may cause pain and you might be crying as of this moment. Stop crying; you are no longer a victim or prisoner of your emotions. You have done the work. Now it is time to release these behaviors and redefine you. Now is the time to become a victor. Now is the time to focus on today and not yesterday. You have to accept what happened; as it happened for you, and not to you.

The External Work: This work will follow you for the rest of your life. Each day you go into the world, obstacles and challenges will come forth and some may make you want to go back to your past. There is nothing in your life today that has anything to do with your childhood abuse so do not allow your past to dominate your present or future. Go out and live. Open yourself to meet new people and don't be afraid of being hurt. Pain and experiences catapult you to the next level of greatness. You can do it. Before we move on to the last Module, I want you to understand how the mind works. There are three levels of consciousness, but I will discuss two.

Conscious Mind – Choice Maker
The three different aspects of the conscious mind are awareness, perception and choices. The primary use of the conscious mind is to make choices. We first have to perceive our environment via the use of our five senses (taste, touch, smell, hear and sight) and that results in awareness. Once we are aware of what we are facing, we can then make choices. Notice your senses are what make you aware.

The Subconscious Mind – Reactive Mind – Beneath Human Level (Animal)
The subconscious mind stores all of your emotions, patterns, learned conditions and behaviors. It also takes up a large amount of space in your mind (80-90%) as compared to our conscious mind (2-10%). The subconscious mind is beneath our true self as it prevents us from moving forward, making great decisions, seeing the truth and succeeding in every area of our lives. Too many of us "live" or dwell in our subconscious and is controlled by it. You will no longer live in your subconscious mind. The subconscious mind is also directly connected to our physical and emotional well-being, and our ability to make conscious choices or decisions. Once we face and remove these learned conditions, emotions, beliefs, patterns and behaviors, we can see clearly; thereby becoming conscious, making better decisions, and living our lives on purpose, and with passion. We can also prevent further manifestation in our physical health as well as our emotional being. This is what I call self-reflection and correction, or removing the clutter; living with a free mind, and cleansed heart.

The subconscious mind **reacts** to triggers. A trigger is something that sets off a memory tape or flashback moving the person back to the event of his/her original trauma. Triggers are very particular; different things trigger different people. Triggers can be something as simple as a candle, an odor, a place, a noise or action, etc., and the emotions associated are buried deep within your subconscious mind. When the pain is not processed, these triggers will always be a big part of your life.

Example:
Your boyfriend has a history of child abuse. You had a disagreement; he disrespected you by calling you out of your name. After he stormed out of the house, you locked the door and put the latch on. He then kicked the door in and broke the latch. You discover later that his abuser locked him in a closet after she raped him.

Explanation:
His behavior of kicking the door in was based on his child molester locking him in a closet after she raped him. The **locking of the closet door** was the **trigger** and he **reacted**. He reacted from **stored emotions surrounding his past abuse** as he did not react from a simple disagreement in the **current situation**. Can you see this?

This is why it is so important to process, manage and control your emotions as the only way to release any trauma is to go back to understand and move forward to live. You do not want to live and be controlled by your subconscious mind or unprocessed past emotions. Your past is a great part of your future as it is a great part of your today. You can either go back and design your life or allow your past to dictate your life.

The last section is the most important as forgiveness is to be set free.
Understanding Sexual Abuse and Other Forms – Knowledge and awareness
The Effects of Abuse – What needs to be transformed
Releasing the Effects of Abuse – Growth and maturity
Move Forward in Forgiveness – Emotional freedom

Module IV – Forgiveness- See Chapter 13

In this module, you will develop an understanding of what Forgiveness is, who it is for, why it is important and the five steps.

Forgiveness is giving up the desire to hurt someone after they have caused you pain. Forgiveness is the last act of love. Forgiveness is a powerful tool because it liberates the soul. As written in Perfectly Planned, forgiveness is letting go of all the pain caused by your abusers. Forgiveness is to become free of the hate, pain and resentment. Forgiveness is the start of a new beginning. What will you gain if you seek revenge, commit suicide, homicide or remained depressed and angry? What will life be like for you? I can assure you happiness is nowhere within reach. Forgiveness is finding peace with all the negative energy that consumed you. Forgiveness is accepting, owning and appreciating your past life. For without it, where will you be? If you love who you are, you have to appreciate your past life. Your past is a part of you and always will be. Your past is not just your past; it should bring you to unconditional self-love and your purpose.

Forgiveness is for you; the victim, not your abuser or wrongdoer. When you walk around angry and bitter, you give your abuser power over you. How? Example…You meet someone new and he or she is well-to-do, respectful and kind, however, your past girlfriend or boyfriend was cold-hearted and cheated on you. Instead of you seeing the new person for who they are, you don't trust him or her because your ex caused you pain. You are giving them power over your emotions and thereby controlling your current relationship because you refuse to "let go", "forgive" your past wrongdoer. You are also living in your subconscious mind.

Why is forgiveness important? Besides the health problems that develop from harboring negative emotions, you will block your blessings. Example: Abuse victims generally do not trust people so imagine if someone new came into your life and you refused to allow them in. Later you discover the purpose of this person was to bless you with a better job, or to meet your husband or wife, or to clean your credit, etc. However, since you don't trust people, you will never know their purpose in your life. What is light without darkness? Embrace the storms and sunny days are always nearby. Un-forgiveness results in everlasting turmoil and self-defeat.

In order to obtain the strength needed to forgive any source of pain; one will have to do the following.

Grieve - Be Sad/Cry
- In most cases when we are hurt by someone we try to suppress the pain. Instead of dealing with it or grieving, we bury it in hopes that it will go away. The problem with that is as long as the pain is present, it will surface and new relationships will be affected. Individuals who have nothing to do with this struggle or pain will feel the wrath from it.
- Without grieving, the heart is bitter and the soul is compromised. By definition I mean, the same pain you felt while being abused or hurt is the same pain that will immediately surface. You will compare every new person and situation to your past instead of looking at the situation for today. A tarnished heart will always retreat to past pain.
- Grieving does not mean going into a depression. It means to have your days of sadness. "Release It" Don't hold on to the pain. *Every tear shed is a sign of strength and freedom to come.* Have your five minutes of self-pity and keep going.

Understanding/Compassion: We have all hurt someone
I know it's difficult to have compassion or understanding for anyone who hurts you, so this is the part of forgiveness that makes it so hard to accomplish. How many times have you hurt someone? We are all human and we all make mistakes. Whether it was intentional or unintentional, we all err. How did you feel after you hurt someone and they held a grudge against you? Deep in your heart you wanted that person to understand your pain and realize you needed deliverance as well. Compassion is your ability to have sympathy for those who cause pain; as hurt people, hurt people. Understand that a happy person does not cause pain, so with that; we must understand that when someone is hurting they can only give off more pain. Have compassion for their suffering.

Accept: Accept that the past will never change
The past can only be accepted and embraced as it will never change. Accept that you were deeply hurt and may be left with scars. It might be difficult to move forward, but you can. You must do the work. Life has many wrongdoers and as long as you live; you will get hurt again. Don't allow that pain to stop you. Understand forgiveness as in doing so, you will live with emotional freedom. You have two choices; live in freedom or in a mental prison. If you choose wisely, I guarantee life gets better. Pain has a purpose and your job is to reach back and find out exactly what that purpose is or was as it always comes with a lesson. That lesson is always to enhance you, not break you.

Accountability: Be responsible for your own actions

When an adult stays in a situation that he/she knows is completely toxic, it is their responsibility to be accountable just as the wrongdoer. That does not imply it was your fault, however, if you knew the situation was bad and you stayed, you are accountable. You have to see who you are, what you allow and what you could have done better. If you know in your heart of hearts you could have made a better decision, you are just as accountable as the wrongdoer. Don't place blame on others when you know you could've done better. Placing blame denies you the opportunity to learn. That leads to repeated history. Denial leads to desolation. Be accountable and accept responsibility and that way you elevate yourself. Example: If you loaned Bob some money and he didn't pay you back, and you loaned him money again and he didn't pay you back. You are accountable as he showed you who he was and you didn't listen. Listen to your inner voice, it knows.

Learn From It: Find something positive

One of the key elements of forgiveness is to learn from the pain. There is a lesson in everything we experience. It doesn't matter how malicious or callus, there is a lesson and a blessing. To learn from hurt is to gain strength. To learn from hurt is to gain knowledge. To learn from hurt is to grow and mature. Find something positive from your experience. Ask yourself, did I learn anything about myself during this experience? Did it make me a better person? What did being abused teach me? Did it teach me to be a better parent than mine? Did it teach me to be skeptical about whom I allow my children to be around? Did it teach me the red flags of an abusive person? Did it teach me to be a writer or speaker? There is a positive in every negative and you can find it, if you seek it. Once you understand forgiveness, being hurt no longer hinders you, it empowers you.

About The Author

A successful leader and expert on overcoming all forms of abuse, avoiding toxic relationships and the art of forgiveness, Kelley Porter is a Certified Transformation, and Personal Development Coach, Award Winning Six-time Author, and Professional Speaker. As a speaker, Kelley's transparent and authentic style of speaking will empower anyone to self-reflect, start the process of healing and correct thoughts and behaviors that may hinder them from living a healthy and non-toxic lifestyle.

As a Coach, Kelley empowers you to reach emotional freedom, gain clarity and discover your infinite possibilities. She is well known for assisting in the removal of mental and emotional blocks that hinders people from reaching their fullest potential. Her areas of specialty are, but not limited to; abuse, healing, relationships, thoughts, emotions, and behaviors as she has written books on all topics. Kelley has over thirty years of direct experience with all forms of abuse, domestic violence relationships, creating purpose and power from painful experiences, and creating a positive mindset.

Kelley contributes to society her genuine love for healing, improving awareness and identity, developing talents and potential; enhancing the quality of life and the realization of dreams and aspirations. Kelley's mission is to guide you to design a healthy and meaningful life through wisdom, consciousness, self-reflection, self-love, accountability and forgiveness. Prior to Kelley discovering her life purpose, she spent twenty-three years in healthcare and worked fifteen of those years as a Medical Technologist, as she is a member of the American Society for Clinical Pathologist.

Kelley has been seen and heard on radio and TV including WVON, HOT105 (Florida), Inspiration 1390, WKKC, Channel 2, 5, 7 and 19 and My Black is Beautiful (online). She has been featured in Rolling Out Magazine, Chicago Tribune, Bean Soup Times, SisterSpeak237 (Africa) and spoken for numerous prestigious organizations such as Robert H. McKinney Law School and the Chicago Police Department. She is available for speaking engagements such as keynotes, seminars, workshops, conferences and panels. Her audience can range from congregations, universities, youth groups, NFP and community organizations, the educational and prison system as well as shelters.

www.ingramcontent.com/pod-product-compliance
Lightning Source LLC
Chambersburg PA
CBHW080520300426
44112CB00018B/2807